M000188913

BOOK ANALYSIS

By Jule Lenzen

Homegoing
BY YAA GYASI

YAA GYASI

GHANAIAN-AMERICAN NOVELIST

- **Born in Mampong, Ghana in 1989.**

Yaa Gyasi was born in Ghana. In 1991 her father was working towards a PhD at the Ohio State University, so the family moved to America and Gyasi was raised in Huntsville, Alabama from the age of ten. She currently lives in Berkeley, California. Before graduating with a Master of Fine Arts degree from the Iowa Writer's Workshop, Gyasi studied English at Stanford University. As a child, she enjoyed reading. After reading Toni Morrison's *Song of Solomon*, she decided to become a writer herself. *Homegoing*, her debut novel, immediately became an international bestseller, and was shortlisted for several literary prizes. It also won the National Book Critics' Circle John Leonard Prize for best first book.

HOMEGOING

A FAMILY HISTORY ABOUT THE DESTRUCTIVE EFFECTS OF COLONIAL RULE AND THE SLAVE TRADE

- **Genre:** novel
- **Reference edition:** Gyasi, Y. (2017) *Homegoing*. UK: Penguin Books.
- **1st edition:** 2016
- **Themes:** Ghana, tribal wars, British colonisation, the slave trade, America, segregation, American Civil War, family history

Homegoing traces the family history of two sisters, Effia and Esi, who never meet. Esi is traded as a slave to the American colonies, meaning her descendants are based in America. Effia is married to a slave trader in Ghana, and her descendants retain the strong connection with Ghana, and, for the most part, live there. Gyasi was largely inspired by the still institutionalised racism she felt growing up in Alabama. She was inspired to write the novel after her first journey to Ghana since leaving the country as a child (*internationales literaturfestival berlin*, 2018). Of the 14 main characters, Marjorie has the strongest autobiographical connections to the author (Hericson: n.p.). Gyasi was also influenced by other works such as African-American author Toni Morrison's *Song of Solomon*, as well as Gabriel García Márquez's *One Hundred Years of Solitude* (*Penguin*, 2017). The novel is divided into two parts: before and after the American Civil War.

SUMMARY

EFFIA AND ESI

Effia, the daughter of Baaba and Cobbe Otcher, is born the night of a terrible fire in Fanteland, Ghana. All her life, she and Baaba have a difficult relationship, and Baaba detests her. Only after the death of her father does Effia learn the truth from her (half)brother Fiifi: she is not really Baaba's child, but that of a maid who ran away during the night of the fire. Effia greatly admires the future leader of the village, Abeeku, and is promised to him in marriage. By a trick, however, Baaba manages to marry Effia to James Collins, the governor of the Castle where the African slaves are held. Effia grows to love him deeply and he seems to care for her as well. However, he also has a wife in England. Effia is horrified by the slave trade that takes place underneath her feet at the Castle. She eventually becomes pregnant by James. Baaba gives Effia a black stone from her real mother when she leaves.

Esi grows up in a village in the Asante nation of Ghana as the daughter of Big Man Asaare and his third wife Maame. She only learns about her sister during her childhood: her mother, Maame, used to be a slave-maid in Fanteland and was raped. She is therefore also against the slave trade in her own village now. One day, a rival clan attacks the village to steal back some of their slaves. Esi is captured and brought to the Castle as a slave herself. She is raped by one of the officers and shipped off to America. She, too, was given a black stone by her mother, but she has to leave it in the Castle.

QUEY AND NESS

Quey is Effia and James' son. Effia is still alive, and the reader learns more about her relationship with James, which seems to have been a happy one. James dies soon after he sends Quey to school in London. He does this as he has discovered the homosexual attraction between Quey and his friend, Cudjo. When Quey returns, he can first continue working at the fort and later is sent to live in his mother's village, to act as a mediator between the locals and the British in the slave trade. His uncle

Fiifi is a major character in the village. Quey also meets Cudjo again, and still has the same feelings for him – he dreams about finally being with him. One day, Fiifi returns from raiding another village: they have captured the Asante princess. Fiifi commands Quey to marry her to strengthen the Fante's position on the Gold Coast, and Quey realises that he has to do his duty.

Ness is Esi's daughter, born during the journey from Ghana to America. She remembers her mother but was separated from her at a young age. Her story picks up when she is working for a farmer in Alabama. There, she forms a close alliance with a little girl named Pinky. It only gradually becomes apparent that Ness was married to another slave, Sam, on her previous farm (whose owner is only ever referred to as the Devil). They had a son together, Kojo, and decided to flee with the help of another slave, Ma Aku. On the run, they were captured, and Sam and Ness sacrificed themselves to save their baby, who managed to escape with Ma Aku. Sam was hanged by the Devil, and Ness was so violently whipped that her back and shoulders bear horrific scars. Later, she was sold to the farm where she meets Pinky and picks cotton.

JAMES AND KOJO

James Richard Collins is the son of Quey and the Asante princess. He is supposed to marry Amma, the daughter of Chief Abeeku, and does marry her to fulfil the family's dream of belonging to the ruling family of the village, which should already have happened in Effia's time. However, on a trip to the Asante nation with his parents, he meets Akosua Mensah and falls in love with her. He promises her to return and states that he feels much more connected to the Asante people of his mother's line, rather than the Fante people of his father's (and Effia's) side. Under a pretext, he travels to the village of Efutu, where he gets involved in the fight between Asante and Fante. He is presumed dead, leaving him free to escape to his life with Akosua. Both Effia and Fiifi are still alive during his lifetime.

Kojo never meets his biological parents, Ness and Sam. He is raised by Ma Aku in Baltimore, where he has been granted the status of a free slave. He is married to Anna, and together they have seven children, with another one on the way, each one's name beginning with the consecutive letters of the alphabet. Their standard of life is greatly improved by the charity of a white family, the Mathisons, who fight for black rights. A law is passed that allows law enforcement to capture all alleged runaways, and one day the heavily pregnant Anna does not return. A decade later, Kojo moves away, to New York.

ABENA AND H

Abena is James and Akosua's daughter. She does not know that she belongs to the royal line of the Asante and her father is only known as 'Unlucky' because he does not have any talent for farming. The family history is cut off here, as Abena never learns about her roots. On a journey to Kumasi, she briefly meets an old man who mistakes her for James. Abena's village has bad harvests and they blame Abena, as she has an affair with Ohene Nyarko, who has promised to marry her once he has had a good harvest. In one year, Ohene introduces cocoa as a plant from another village, and it produces the first good harvest in years. However, Ohene does not marry Abena, as he promised to marry the daughter of the man who sold him the cocoa seeds. Abena flees to a Christian missionary church in Kumasi.

Between the chapters of Abena and H, part two of the book begins, meaning that everything from H's chapter onwards deals with the time after the American Civil War. In H's chapter, the reader learns what happened to Anna: she was captured and killed herself, and baby H had to be cut out of her dead body in order to save his life. H grows up on a farm in the South and is free after the Civil War. He is then forcefully conscripted to work in the coal mines, where he spends most of his adult life. Once he is free, he moves to Pratt City and writes to the love of his youth, Ethe, who joins him shortly after. H never meets the rest of his family and has no idea that he has seven siblings and a father, who are presumably still alive for a major part of his life. His father maybe even lives in New York at the same time as he does. Like in Effia's line, the family history here suffers a complete cut.

AKUA AND WILLIE

Akua grows up in the missionary church that her mother took refuge in. She cannot relate to the Christian teachings; instead, a local medicine man is her role model. Later, she learns that the

Missionary accidentally killed her mother when he tried to baptise her in the river. He burned her corpse and all her belongings. Akua is married to Asamoah and has three children, two daughters and a son. She is traumatised when she sees the villagers burning a white man, and keeps seeing a firewoman in her dreams, holding two fire children. There is also a war between the tribes and the British, from which Akua's husband returns one-legged. One night, Akua sleepwalks, sets the hut on fire, and burns her children – her husband only manages to rescue baby Yaw, their son. From then on, the villagers call her 'Crazy Woman'. The Missionary eventually returns her black stone necklace to her.

Willie's story picks up when she is living with two children in Harlem, a part of New York. In retrospect she recounts her love story with Richard, who grew up with her in Pratt City. His skin tone is very light, and when he moves with Willie and their baby, Carson, to New York after the death of Willie's parents, he realises that the white population accepts him as one of their own. The spouses drift apart, and one fateful night they meet by accident in the club where Willie works as a cleaner. Richard is forced to have sex with her while his colleagues watch, and afterwards leaves. Willie sees him one more time, and he seems to have remarried, this time with a white woman, whom he has a child with. Willie later starts a relationship with Eli, whom she meets at church. He is a poet and is often absent for months at a time. They have a baby together, Josephine. Willie has a talent for singing, the reason she originally moved to Harlem, and at the end of her story, she starts to sing gospels at the church.

YAW AND SONNY

Yaw is a teacher at a school in Ghana. He is already middle-aged and defined by the scar on his cheek that he got as a baby. He does not believe he will ever find love, and lives far away from home and his mother, 'Crazy Woman'. Eventually, he gets a housemaid, Ethe, and after a few years they travel together to see Akua. In Yaw's chapter, Akua finally gets to explain her dreams and the story of their ancestry is unravelled. Yaw is in love with Ethe but has not declared himself yet when the chapter ends.

Willie is still a strong presence in Sonny's life. He spends his life in Harlem, and first campaigns for black equal rights, which he is constantly arrested for. However, after a while he gives up. He meets Amani, who is a heroin addict, and becomes addicted himself. In the end, however, Willie convinces him to give the drug up.

MARJORIE AND MARCUS

Marjorie grows up in Alabama in the US, the child of Ethe and Yaw, who has become a professor at the university. She travels yearly to Ghana, and her grandmother Akua is a strong presence in her life. From her, she learns the history of her ancestors. She differs from the other African-American children in her school, as she is a first-generation immigrant and does not carry around the history of slavery. She has a brief affair with a white boy, Graham, at her school, but his parents forbid him from going out with her because of her skin colour. At the end of the chapter, her grandmother dies, and she is devastated.

For Marcus, both Willie and Sonny are important characters in his childhood. At one point, he is rescued by them after being abducted by his heroin-addicted mother Amani. Marcus ends up studying at Stanford, where he does a PhD. in sociology, trying to write about the forceful conscription of black people to the mines. Marcus meets Marjorie at a party and they become close friends, bonding over their shared interest in Ghana. They travel there together, and Marcus is the first person in his family line since Esi to return to his homeland. He and Marjorie fight their demons together: Marcus is afraid of the ocean and Marjorie of fire, probably just like their ancestors, Effia and Esi.

CHARACTER STUDY

The novel has 14 main characters in total, and many supporting characters in addition to that. Therefore, in this section, only two characters will be analysed in depth: Kojo from Esi's line and Akua from Effia's line. These have been selected as they are crucial to the further development of the novel's themes.

KOJO

Kojo is the son of Ness and Sam, who escaped the slave owner called the Devil with the help of Ma Aku. He grows up under her care in Baltimore, where they both get granted the status of free slave. Ma Aku is like a mother to Kojo, and they are very close. She also lives with him when he is married to Anna, who was born free: he and Anna have seven children, and Anna is pregnant with another, baby H. Kojo works on the docks in Baltimore, and tries to evade police attention as much as possible, as black people are much more likely to get arrested. He is a good and reliable worker and looks after his family, and he is devoted to his wife and their children. He tries to be a good father, as he never got to know his own. Kojo and his family live under the protection of the white Mathisons, who fight for black rights. Kojo himself stays out of politics. He is very friendly, no matter what skin colour another person has, and he loves the city of Baltimore.

He breaks apart when Anna disappears. He is not a good father to his children any more and becomes extremely depressed. Once his children have moved out and Ma Aku is dead, Kojo leaves the city and moves to New York.

AKUA

Akua is one of the most present characters in the novel: she is mentioned in her own chapter, and in the chapters of Yaw, Marjorie and Marcus. She has visions, and it is thanks to her that Marjorie knows about her ancestors.

Akua is the daughter of Abena and Ohene Nyarko, although she never gets to know the identity of her father. She grows up at the missionary church in Kumasi, but she is more impressed by the teachings of the local witch doctor. She leaves the church to marry Asamoah and learns that her mother's corpse was burned by the priest who accidentally killed her. This probably sparks off Akua's enduring fear of fire. She does not enjoy cooking, and seeing her fellow villagers burn a white man at the stake makes matters even worse. She begins to have visionary dreams of a fire woman and her two fire children (referring to her ancestor Maame and her two daughters Effia and Esi) and is terrified of going to sleep. While sleepwalking, Akua burns the hut containing her two daughters, Abee and Ama Serwah. She loves her children and is devastated, and never forgives herself for what she has done (p. 242). Her son Yaw survives, but he does not talk to her until he himself is a middle-aged man. By that point, Akua has become more lucid than she was when she first started to have the dreams: she explains to Yaw, and later to her granddaughter Marjorie, that she has been seeing the story of their ancestors. Akua has an instinct for the supernatural, which she describes as her "growing ear" (p. 177)

She also gives the family heirloom, the black stone necklace, to Marjorie. They are extremely close and Marjorie visits her once a year in Ghana, where Akua lives close to the Castle where her ancestors were sold as slaves. Akua has various nicknames during her lifetime: 'Crazy Woman' and 'Old Lady'. She dies in her sleep and is buried on a mountain overlooking the Ghanaian sea.

ANALYSIS

THE FIRE IMAGE

One of the images that recurs throughout the novel is that of fire. It begins in the very first generation, with Effia being born the night of a fire:

> "The night Effia Otcher was born [...], a fire raged through the woods just outside her father's compound. It moved quickly, tearing a path for days. It lived off the air; it slept in caves and hid in trees; it burned, up and through, unconcerned with what wreckage it left behind, until it reached an Asante village. There, it disappeared, becoming one with the night." (p. 3)

The fire is given properties that make it sound like it is alive, which leads to the assumption that the fire might indeed stand for Maame, as she also runs off after giving birth to Effia and settles in an Asante village. Maame also later appears as firewoman to Akua (p. 267), and says herself that she set a fire (p. 42). The importance of the fire is further emphasised at the start of the novel:

> "He [Cobbe Otcher] knew then that the memory of the fire that burned, that fled, would haunt him, his children, and his children's children for as long as the line continued. [...] The villagers began to say that the baby was born of the fire [...]." (p. 4)

This image is taken up time and again in the subsequent generations, most notably in the story of Akua, who sees Maame as the firewoman with two fire children. Even before her dreams, Akua is scared of fire. So is Yaw, her son, and Marjorie, her granddaughter. A connection to fire, albeit a less obvious one, can even be seen in Esi's line: H works his entire life in the coal mines.

The novel also closes with fire, namely with Marjorie overcoming her fear of it:

> "She walked to where he stood, where the fire met the water. He took her hand and they both looked out into the abyss of it. The fear that Marcus had felt inside the Castle was still there, but he knew it was like the fire, a wild thing that could still be controlled, contained." (p. 300)

In a way, the story has come full circle through the reunion of Effia and Esi's descendants. Marjorie and Marcus have opposing fears of water and fire, and indeed the water image is also taken up on several occasions throughout the novel. For example, Ma Aku, who raises Kojo in Baltimore, still remembers her homeland of Ghana, and for her, water symbolises the connection to her home country: "She could often be found looking out at the water, looking as if she would jump in, try to find her way home." (p. 113). It is the fire that separated the family line, but the ocean, or water, is what separated one branch of the family from their homeland.

The connection between fire and water is already drawn in Esi's story, when Little Dove says:

> "[...] You are not your mother's first daughter. There was one before you. And in my village we have a saying about separated sisters. They are like a woman and her reflection, doomed to stay on opposite sides of the pond." (pp. 38-39)

THE BLACK STONE

Both Effia and Esi are given a certain stone by Maame: "[...] a black stone pendant that shimmered as though it was coated in gold dust." (p. 16). Together with the fire image, this is a theme that spans the whole novel. Both are connected, particularly in Akua's story:

> "[...] He dropped the necklace very suddenly and said, 'Do you know there is evil in your lineage? [...] this thing you are carrying, it does not belong to you.' When I told him about my dreams, he said that the firewoman was an ancestor come back to visit me. He said that the black stone had belonged to her and that is why it grew hot in his hand. [...]" (p. 241)

This is the stone that Effia gives to her descendants. The two images are further interconnected in Akua's story, as the priest burns all her mother's belongings apart from the stone.

Esi's stone, however, never leaves Ghana: she is forced to hide it in the Castle and is transported so suddenly to America that she does not manage to take it with her. This leaves her with no family heirloom to give to her descendants, and no connection to her home country. This violent separation is reflected in the violent founding of her family line: her daughter Ness is the result of her rape by a white soldier.

In contrast to this, Effia's line is founded on love and the mutual wish for children. Both family lines, however, receive interruptions. H has no idea who his ancestors were. In a way, then, the stone image serves to show the disruptiveness of the history of slavery. The only time the stone leaves Effia's line is also through white, colonial intervention – the Missionary keeps it before giving it to Akua. Therefore, in this context, the absence of the stone is also caused by the disruptive nature of colonialism. In Effia's line, however, the black stone necklace always finds its way back to the family members, and it serves as a powerful connection to their Ghanaian past and to Effia. In the end, Marjorie is aware of her full family history. Marcus, however, has no idea where he came from prior to his great-grandfather H.

Marcus and Marjorie are the first members of the two lines to meet – they return to Ghana, and their union (both of the family, and with the long-lost homeland) seems to have a healing effect. This union is also symbolised through Marjorie's giving Marcus her stone necklace:

"'Here,' Marjorie said. 'Have it.' She lifted the stone from her neck, 'and placed it around Marcus's. 'Welcome home.' He felt the stone hit his chest, hard and hot, before finding its way up to the surface again. He touched it, surprised by its weight." (p. 300)

TIME

On her novel, Gyasi says: "I felt as though each new chapter, each new character, was itself a kind of crossroads, moving along a path that had already been laid out to some degree by the choices of the chapter before, the ancestors" (Hericson: n.p.). She shows how the histories of slavery and colonialism are still informing the present.

The problems Gyasi addresses earlier in the novel accumulate in the last two chapters on Marjorie and Marcus. Racism, both by whites and within the black community, and a feeling of rootlessness are both central topics. Marcus expresses this as follows:

"And if he slammed the book down, then everyone in the room would stare and all they would see would be his skin and his anger, and they'd think they knew something about him, and it would be the same something that had justified putting his great-grandpa H in prison, only it would be different too, less obvious than it once was." (pp. 289-90)

Here, Marcus clearly shows how the history of slavery informs a present of internalised racism. Marcus also has trouble writing his PhD thesis because he is preoccupied with the interconnectedness of the history of slavery: he finds it impossible to concentrate on one isolated fact, as every event in the history of discrimination against black Americans seems to be interconnected (p. 289).

On the Ghanaian side, this interconnectedness is partly expressed through an inherited fear of fire. Moreover, Akua speaks out on the effects of colonial rule on the Ghanaian community:

"What I know now, my son: Evil begets evil. It grows. It transmutes, so that sometimes you cannot see that the evil in the world began as the evil in your own home. [...] When someone does wrong, whether it is you or me, whether it is mother or father, whether it is the Gold Coast man or the white man, it is like a fisherman

> casting a net into the water. He keeps only the
> one or two fish that he needs to feed himself
> and puts the rest in the water, thinking that now
> their lives will go back to normal. No one forgets
> that they were once captive, even if they are now
> free. [...]" (p. 242)

This statement can also be applied to the history of slavery in America and underlines Marcus' observation on internalised racism. Similar to the inherited fear of fire in Effia's line, Kojo's daughter is plagued by nightmares, which reflect her ancestors' history of slavery:

> "Beulah was running. Maybe this is where it
> started, Jo thought. Maybe Beulah was seeing
> something more clearly on the nights she had
> these dreams, a little black child fighting in her
> sleep against an opponent she couldn't name
> come morning because in the light the opponent
> looked just like the world around her." (p. 120)

Gyasi herself points out that she chose the format of her novel to be able to underline the interconnectedness of history: "[...] I felt that I need a structure that could accommodate the weight of as many years as possible, so I decided to tell the story generationally" (Hericson: n.p.).

FURTHER REFLECTION

SOME QUESTIONS TO THINK ABOUT...

- Why do you think Marjorie gives the stone, a family heirloom, to Marcus? Is it because she realises they are kin? Or for some other reason? Explain your answer.

- Both family lines are disrupted on several occasions. For example, James runs away from his family, and his direct descendants never learn of their royal heritage. On the other side, once Kojo is separated from his mother Ness, he has no idea about his true homeland. Do you think there is more of a connection in Effia's family line than there is in Esi's, reflected through the presence/absence of the family heirloom? Explain your answer.

- Do you think Marcus has the gift of vision as well, just like Akua? Consider the passage on p. 290.

- Many of the reviews of the novel highlight it as 'the story of America', or 'the impact of slave trade on America', thereby sidelining the

Ghanaian side of the novel completely. Why is that, do you think?

- Following on from the previous question, do you believe that the novel favours the American side of history? Consider also the splitting of the novel in before and after the American Civil War.
- Despite the difference in history, what parallels can you see in the two family lines? Support your answer with examples from the text.
- Following on from the previous question, do you think some of these parallels show how both slavery and colonial rule have the same effect on their victims? Consider also Akua's statement (p. 242) in this context.
- James Richard Collins says that he feels a lot more connected to the line of his mother, the Asante princess, than to that of his father, which would be the line of Effia (p. 102). Why do you think that is?
- What do you think is meant by 'the Evil' that Akua refers to in her own family line (p. 242)? Explain your answer.

We want to hear from you!
Leave a comment on your online library
and share your favourite books on social media!

FURTHER READING

REFERENCE EDITION

- Gyasi, Y. (2017) *Homegoing*. UK: Penguin Books.

REFERENCE STUDIES

- (2017) The books that influenced Yaa Gyasi. *Penguin*. [Online]. [Accessed 20 February 2019]. Available from: <https://www.penguin.co.uk/articles/2017/books-that-influenced-yaa-gyasi.html>

- (2018) Yaa Gyasi [Ghana, USA]. *internationales literaturfestival berlin*. [Online]. [Accessed 13 February 2019]. Available from: <http://literaturfestival.com/autoren/autoren-2017/yaa.gyasi.ldw>

- Hericson, S. (No date) Questions & Answers. *Foyles*. [Online]. [Accessed 13 February 2019]. Available from: <https://www.foyles.co.uk/Author-Yaa-Gyasi>

ADDITIONAL SOURCES

- The Editors of Encyclopaedia Britannica. (2017) Asante. *Encyclopaedia Britannica*. [Online].

[Accessed 26 February 2019]. Available from: <https://www.britannica.com/topic/Asante>

- The Editors of Encyclopaedia Britannica. (2017) Fante. *Encyclopaedia Britannica*. [Online]. [Accessed 26 February 2019]. Available from: <https://www.britannica.com/topic/Fante>

- Kolchin, P. (1995) *American Slavery: 1619-1877*. London: Penguin Books.

- Salm, S. J. and Falola, T. (2002) *Culture and Customs of Ghana*. Westport, CT: Greenwood Press.

www.brightsummaries.com

Ebook EAN: 9782808018791

Paperback EAN: 9782808018807

Legal Deposit: D/2019/12603/106

Cover: © Primento

Digital conception by Primento, the digital partner of
publishers.

Made in the USA
Columbia, SC
14 June 2023